"哈！你找到什么啦？"
Ah! What did you find?

For a FREE audio reading and other bilingual books visit:
www.AuthorJoyMeng.com

Follow us

@AuthorJoyMeng

Copyright © 2021 Xingyu Meng. All rights reserved. No part of this book may be reproduced or used in any manner without the prior written permission of the copyright owner, except for the use of brief quotations in a book review. To request permissions, contact the publisher at authorjoymeng@gmail.com
Edited by Editor Arn Jones-Coney. Art and Layout by Artist Grace Fu. Printed in the USA.
First paperback edition November 2021.
Library of Congress Control Number: 2021922548
ISBN 978-1-956485-01-1

liǎng kē dòu zǐ
兩顆豆子
Two Beans

By Anya Meng Galappatty & Dr. Joy Meng
Illustrated by Grace Fu.

句子

wǒ xǐ huān	
我喜欢……	I like……

wǒ bú xǐ huān	
我不喜欢……	I don't like……

wǒ yǒu	
我有……	I have……

wǒ méi yǒu	
我没有……	I don't have……

wǒ shí me yě méi yǒu！	
我什么也没有！……	I have nothing. Nothing comes out for me!

dàizhe zhè gè wèn tí dú zhè gè gù shì:
带着这个问题读这个故事：
Read this story and ask yourself this question:

nǎ yī kē dòu zǐ de yá gèng duō?
哪一颗豆子的芽更多？
Which bean sprouted more buds?

wǒ men wán zhǒng dòu zǐ ba
我们玩种豆子吧？
Do you want to play growing bean?

zěn me wán
怎么玩？
How?

kàn shuí de dòu zi de yá duō
看谁的豆子的芽多！
Let's see which bean sprouts the most buds!

hǎo
好
Okey!

wǒ xǐ huān hóng dòu
我喜欢红豆!
I like the red bean!

lǜ dòu
绿豆,
Green bean,

zhè me xiǎo
这么小!
It is so small……

wǒ yě xǐ huān hóng dòu
我也喜欢红豆!
I also like the red bean! It is big!

hóng dòu dà
红豆大!
It is big!

bù! hóng dòu shì wǒ de
不!红豆是我的
No! The red bean is mine!

nǐ yǒu lán yī fú
你有蓝衣服！
You have blue clothes!

nǐ yǒu fěn hóng qún zǐ
你有粉红裙子！
You have pink skirts!

nǐ hái yǒu cǎi sè tóu fā
你还有彩色头发！
You have colorful hair also!

nǐ shén me dōu yǒu
你什么都有！
You have everything!

wǒ lián tóu fā dōu méi yǒu
我连头发都没有！
I even have no hair!

hǎo ba　　gěi nǐ
好吧！给你！
Fine! Take the red bean then!

xiè xiè
谢谢！
Thanks!

hóng dòu dà, yá yá duō
红豆大，芽芽多！
This red bean is big. It will sprout a lot of buds!

lǜ dòu xiǎo, xiǎo yá yá gèng duō
绿豆小，小芽芽更多！
This green bean is small. It will sprout more small buds!

wǒ gěi xiǎo lǜ dòu jiāo shuǐ
我给小绿豆浇水！
I water the small green bean!

wǒ gěi dà hóng dòu jiāo shuǐ
我给大红豆浇水！
I water the big red bean!

浇水！
浇水！
浇水！

wǒ duì xiǎo lǜ dòu shuō : "kuài fā yá"
我对小绿豆说:"快发芽。"
I tell the small green bean: "Sprout."

wǒ duì dà hóng dòu shuō : kuài fā yá
我对大红豆说:快发芽!
I tell the big red bean: "Sprout!"

快发芽!
快发芽!
快发芽!

wǒ duì tā chàng gē
我对它唱歌。
I sing to it.

wǒ duì tā chàng gē tiào wǔ
我对它唱歌、跳舞！
I sing and dance to it!

wǒ de huā pén
我的花盆！
My flowerpot!

啪！

把你的花盆给我！
bǎ nǐ de huā pén gěi wǒ

Give your flowerpot to me!

不！
bù
No!

nín nòng huài le wǒ de huā pén
您弄坏了我的花盆！
You broke my flowerpot!

wǒ bù gēn nǐ wán le
我不跟你玩了！
I don't want to play with you!

nà
那……
Err...

gěi wǒ
给我！
Give it to me!

wǒ méi yǒu huā pén le
我没有花盆了！
I don't have a flowerpot then!

wǎn
碗！
A bowl!

wǒ bù xǐ huān wǎn
我不喜欢碗！
I don't like a bowl!

wǒ xǐ huān huā pén
我喜欢花盆！
I like a folwerpot!

zhè shì huā wǎn
这是花碗！
This is a flower bowl!

hǎo ba
好吧。
Okey.

第一个星期
dì yī gè xīng qī
Week 1

wǒ yǒu yī piàn xiǎo lǜ yá
我有一片小绿芽!
I have one small green bud!

wǒ shén me yě méi yǒu
我什么也没有!
Nothing comes out for me!

wǒ yǒu liǎng piàn xiǎo lǜ yá
我有两片小绿芽！
I have two small green buds!

wǒ shén me yě méi yǒu
我什么也没有！
Nothing comes out for me!

wǒ yào yíng le
我要赢了！
I am going to win!

wǒ bù xǐ huān wǎn
我不喜欢碗！
I don't like this bowl!

第三个星期
Week 3

wǒ yǒu sān piàn xiǎo lǜ yá
我有三片小绿芽！
I have three small green buds!

wǒ shén me yě méi yǒu
我什么也没有
Nothing comes out for me!

dì sì gè xīng qī
第四个星期
Week 4

wǒ yǒu sì piàn xiǎo lǜ yá
我有四片小绿芽!
I have four small green buds!

wǒ shén me yě méi yǒu
我什么也没有!
Nothing comes out for me!

<pre>
wǒ yǒu wǔ piàn xiǎo lǜ yá
</pre>
我有五片小绿芽！
I have five small green buds!

<pre>
wǒ shén me yě méi yǒu
</pre>
我什么也没有！
Nothing comes out for me!

第六个星期
Week 6

wǒ yǒu liù piàn dà hóng yá
我有六片大红芽！！！！！！
I have six big red buds!!!!!!

hái shì liù piàn xiǎo lǜ yá
还是六片小绿芽……
Still six tiny green buds...

wǒ de dà shén dòu
我的大神豆！
My big magic bean!！！Aha! Aha! Aha! Aha!!

yī yè zhǎng chū liù piàn
一 夜 长 出 六 片！
The six buds grew in one night!

ā hā! wǒ zhī dào le.
啊哈！我知道了。
Aha! I get it.

yǒu de dòu zǐ zǎo diǎn fā yá yǒu de dòu zǐ wǎn diǎn fā yá
有的豆子早点发芽。有的豆子晚点发芽。
Some beans sprout earlier. Some sprout later.

yǒu de fā dà yá   yǒu de fā xiǎo yá
有的发大芽，有的发小芽。
Some beans sprout big buds. Some sprout tiny buds.

yǒu de fā lǜ yá   yǒu de fā hóng yá
有的发绿芽，有的发红芽。
Some beans sprout green buds. Some sprout red buds.

shì dòu zǐ zǒng huì fā yá
是豆子总会发芽！
As long as they are beans, they will sprout!

lǜ dòu
绿豆。
Green bean.

lǜ huā
绿花？
Green flowers?

献给我们的阳光

Dad Sampath Galappatty

Neighbor Kanika Keo

Friend Na Lin

十个问题

1. 这个故事讲了什么？
   What was the story about?

2. 蛋蛋遇到了什么问题？
   What was Dani's problem?

3. 这个问题是怎么解决的？
   How was Dani's problem resolved?

4. 你喜欢这个故事吗？为什么？
   Did you like the story? Why?

5. 安安和蛋蛋种了几颗豆子？
   How many beans did Aanya and Dani plant?

   A. 两颗   B. 三颗
   Two   Three

6. 故事一开始，蛋蛋为什么喜欢红豆？
Why did Dani want the red bean at the beginning?

A. 喜欢红色
Like red color.

B. 红豆大
The red bean is big.

7. 第一个星期，哪一颗豆子长出了一片芽？
In the first week, which bean sprouted one bud?

A. 绿豆
Green bean

B. 红豆
Red bean

8. 前五个星期，哪一颗豆子发出了更多的芽？
In the first five weeks, which bean sprouted more buds?

A. 绿豆
Green bean

B. 红豆
Red bean

9. 第六个星期，哪一颗豆子一夜长出六片芽？
In the sixth week, which bean sprouted six buds in one night?

A. 绿豆
Green bean

B. 红豆
Red bean

ān ān zhī dào le shén me
10. 安安知道了什么？
What was Aanya aware?

shì dòu zǐ zǒng huì fā yá de
A. 是豆子总会发芽的。
As long as they are beans, they will sprout.

lǜ dòu bǐ hóng dòu hǎo
B. 绿豆比红豆好。
Green beans are better than red beans.

hóng dòu bǐ lǜ dòu hǎo
C. 红豆比绿豆好。
Red beans are better than green beans.

zǎo fā yá bǐ wǎn fā yá hǎo
D. 早发芽比晚发芽好。
It's better to sprout earlier than later.

dá àn
答案
Answers

5.A   6.B   7.A   8.A   9.B   10.A

Aanya Meng Galappatty

is an American-born Asian girl. She was born in Boston, Massachusetts in 2015 and grew up in a multicultural family. On a daily basis, she speaks Chinese and English two different languages. She loves writing poems, painting, playing the piano and playing outside with her friends. Her dream is to travel to the Panda Hotel in Guangzhou, China with her three panda toys: Noodle, Rice and Dumpling!

Dr. Joy Meng

is a Chinese-American mom, a native Chinese speaker, and a Chinese teacher with a PhD in Chinese Literatures and Arts. When visiting local libraries in Massachusetts, her daughter Aanya and she had trouble finding well-illustrated, funny and meaningful Chinese picture books for children. Because of this, she decided to create the "Life with Aanya" series in 201 and shared them with all mothers and daughters around the world!

Grace Fu

Telling stories to children through illustrations is what she loves to do. She also collects well-illustrated children's picture books from different places around the world. She enjoys illustrating children's stories because the colors are bright and cheerful, the shapes are simple and cute, and she can make the scenes fresh and sweet!

Made in the USA
Middletown, DE
16 October 2022